THE PLAYS

Brooke Berman

BROADWAY PLAY PUBLISHING INC
224 E 62nd St, NY NY 10065-8201
212 772-8334 fax: 212 772-8358
BroadwayPlayPubl.com

THE LIDDY PLAYS
© Copyright 2012 by Brooke Berman

First printing: August 2012
Second printing: August 2013
I S B N: 978-0-88145-544-1

Book design: Marie Donovan
Page make-up: Adobe Indesign
Typeface: Palatino
Printed and bound in the U S A

ABOUT THE AUTHOR

Brooke Berman is an award-winning playwright
and screenwriter. Originally trained as an actor and
solo performer in the experimental theater, Brooke
began performing her own work on the Lower East
Side of Manhattan before receiving formal training
in playwriting from the Juilliard School. Her play
HUNTING AND GATHERING, which premiered
at Primary Stages, directed by Leigh Silverman, was
named one of the Ten Best of 2008 by *New York*. Her
memoir, *No Place Like Home*, published by Random
House, was released in June, 2010 and named both
"Highbrow" and "Brilliant" by *New York*'s Approval
Matrix. The book made Elle.com's "Top Ten Summer
Reads" and was featured in *Los Angeles*'s summer
reading roundup.

Brooke's plays have been produced and developed
across the U S at theaters including: Primary Stages,
The Second Stage, Steppenwolf, The Play Company,
Soho Rep, Williamstown Theater Festival, Naked
Angels, M C C, WET, S P F, New Dramatists, New
Georges, The Hourglass Group, and the Eugene
O'Neill Theater Center. In the U K, her work has
been developed at The Royal Court Theatre, The
National Theatre Studio, and Pentabus. Plays include:
HUNTING AND GATHERING (Primary Stages);
SMASHING (The Play Company, The O'Neill); UNTIL
WE FIND EACH OTHER (Steppenwolf, The O'Neill);

THE TRIPLE HAPPINESS (Second Stage), SAM AND LUCY (S P F, Cleveland Playhouse), A PERFECT COUPLE (WET), OUT OF THE WATER (Cape Cod Theater Project, ARS Nova), CASUAL ENCOUNTERS (New Dramatists Creativity Fund) and others. Her plays are published by Broadway Play Publishing Inc, Playscripts, Backstage Books, and Smith & Kraus.

Brooke is the recipient of a Berilla Kerr Award, a Helen Merrill Award, two Francesca Primus Awards, two LeComte du Nuoy awards, and a commissioning grant from the National Foundation for Jewish Culture. She was a playwright in residence at New Dramatists, where she served on the Board of Directors. She has received support for her work from the MacDowell Colony and the Corporation of Yaddo.

Her short play DANCING WITH A DEVIL was a co-winner of The Heideman Award at Actors Theater of Louisville in 1999, presented in "Life Under 30" at the Humana Festival, and nominated for an American Theater Critics Best New Play award.

Brooke attended Barnard College and was a Lila Acheson Wallace Playwriting Fellow and writer in residence at The Juilliard School. She is a member of the Dramatists Guild, PEN and the M C C Playwrights Coalition.

More information: www.brookeberman.net

THE LIDDY PLAYS, PARTS ONE, TWO, AND THREE was originally workshopped with Clubbed Thumb at HERE Theater, New York, NY in their Summerworks festival in 1999. The cast and creative contributor were:

LIDDY/MOM .... Monica Koskey
STEPHEN/ROBERT/MEDITATION
INSTRUCTOR .... Trevor Williams
EMERSON ....Benjamin Krevolin
SUSAN/SOCIAL WORKER .... Mariana Newhard

Director .... Tim Farrell

PART FOUR was written in 2000. The play was then developed in its entirety at Rising Phoenix Rep in residence at Walker Space in August 2001. The cast and creative contributor were:

LIDDY.. Aidan Sullivan
STEPHEN/ROBERT.. Robert Beitzel
EMERSON .... Michael Goldstrom
SUSAN/SOCIAL WORKER .... Addie Johnson
CARLA..Yvonne Woods
MOM .... Caren Browning

Director .... Michael Barakiva

There was a subsequent workship at Rattlestick Theater in December 2001. The cast and creative contrbutor were:

LIDDY.. Aidan Sullivan
STEPHEN ....Robert Beitzel
EMERSON .... Michael Chernus
SUSAN/SOCIAL WORKER ....Jenny Ikeda
CARLA..Yvonne Woods
MOM .... Caren Browning

Director..Michael Barakiva

The play was then done with the Williamstown Theater Festival non-Equity company, in 2005,

LIDDY/MOM ....Eliza Baldi
STEPHEN ....James McMenamin
EMERSON ....Michael Braun
SUSAN .... Erin McMonagle
ROBERT/SOCIAL WORKER ....Louis Chanchien
CARLA... Niki Berger

Director.. Johanna McKeon

CHARACTERS & SETTING

LIDDY, *a precocious young woman*
EMERSON, *her older brother*
STEPHEN, *a young man in a psych ward, a mad poet*
SUSAN, EMERSON's *college girlfriend. From a very good home.*
ROBERT, *a high school guidance counselor*
CARLA, *a Vipassana meditation instructor*
MOM, *beautiful and crazy. A ghost in yellow.*

Part One: The Bay Area, CA

Part Two: Chicago, IL

Part Three: Palo Alto, CA

Part Four: Seattle, WA

note: the structure is deliberately open and scenes should flow in and out of one another effortlessly.

the liddy plays

part one

liddy and the mad hatter

(LIDDY *and* EMERSON *in separate areas onstage.*)

LIDDY: It was craziness.

EMERSON: We took it for granted.

LIDDY: It was just Mom. We had always known her like that—

EMERSON: Mom was the Universe—

LIDDY: —and the Universe functioned by rules that were mysterious, by movements we could not understand. So it was Mom being Mom, and God being God—

EMERSON: —we did not think that anything was wrong, really—

LIDDY: —except that it all felt kind of wrong, and later when we grew up we saw that the world of our house and the world of our Mom didn't quite correspond to the rules of the world outside the family—

EMERSON: —and we came to see that our mom was different than other moms.

LIDDY: It wasn't that she was eccentric either. I think now that she would be called *borderline something or other,* but back then emotionally unstable middle class women were not diagnosed as schizo-effective—

EMERSON: They were labelled difficult and encouraged to shop.

LIDDY: Mom got treated with bad therapy, valium and husbands. The husbands ran out as often as the prescriptions.

EMERSON: She wasn't easy to live with.

LIDDY: And, anyway, then she died, and as horrible as it sounds, I think, my brother and I were kind of relieved.

EMERSON: I wouldn't say "relieved".

LIDDY: I would. Sort of. I mean, it's complicated. But, I would.

(Lights fade on EMERSON and rise on LIDDY"s space as LIDDY takes the story—)

LIDDY: I went into social work because the one thing I knew I was good at was dealing with crazy people. I had been trained by the best.

(Lights down on EMERSON and up on STEPHEN.)

LIDDY: Stephen was my age.

STEPHEN: Twenty-eight.

LIDDY: I don't know why, but that mattered. He'd checked himself into the hospital where I was doing my social work residency.
The morning after he first arrived, the doctors asked "Do you think you're in touch with reality?" and he said:

STEPHEN: I went to Yale. We were taught that reality is subjective.

LIDDY: And they said, That's not going to help you here. I started to spend time with him just after that.

liddy meets stephen

LIDDY: I'm Liddy Green.

STEPHEN: Yes?

LIDDY: Can you talk?

STEPHEN: Yes.

LIDDY: Do you know why you're here?

STEPHEN: Yes. I checked myself in.

LIDDY: Right. But do you... Why do you think you did that?

STEPHEN: Because I thought I was going crazy and this seemed like a good place to do that.

LIDDY: Are you going crazy?

STEPHEN: I don't know. Am I?

LIDDY: I don't know. Are you?

STEPHEN: You're not very helpful.

LIDDY: Well. I mean, I—

STEPHEN: I mean, you don't know a lot.

LIDDY: It's the mind. No one knows a lot about the mind.

STEPHEN: So I hear.

LIDDY: We can't ascertain what your experience is. You have to tell us things.

STEPHEN: I hear that too. Ascertain is a good word.

LIDDY: Thank you. I like it.

STEPHEN: So what were you asking?

LIDDY: If you think you're crazy?

STEPHEN: Oh, right. That. I don't know if I'm crazy.

LIDDY: I hear you hear voices.

STEPHEN: Who do you hear that from?

LIDDY: Ha ha.

STEPHEN: I did hear—A voice. I haven't since I've been here.

LIDDY: The medication—

STEPHEN:—Kills it.

LIDDY: Yes. I'm going to be here a lot. If you want to talk.

STEPHEN: Okay.

LIDDY: Anything you want to talk about. Anything.

STEPHEN: Lets talk about you.

LIDDY: Okay. What do you want to know about me?

STEPHEN: Do you feel pain that is not your own?

LIDDY: No. My own pain has been pretty sufficient.

STEPHEN: I feel pain for the whole world only the world doesn't know it's in pain and I do.

LIDDY: I think the world is starting to catch on.

STEPHEN: Have you felt that?

LIDDY: Pain?

STEPHEN: No. Pain for the world.

LIDDY: I don't think I differentiate.

STEPHEN: I see.

LIDDY: Do you feel pain that _is_ your own?

STEPHEN: I don't know that I believe in private ownership. Of anything.

LIDDY: I see. Is there anything you need?

STEPHEN: I don't know.

LIDDY: If you did need something, what would it be?

STEPHEN: Water.

LIDDY: Good. What would the water do?

STEPHEN: It would make my mouth less dry. It's practical. The meds make my mouth dry.

LIDDY: Oh. Right. Of course they do. So, you were being literal.

STEPHEN: As opposed to figurative?

LIDDY: Well, yes.

STEPHEN: Liddy, I am very dry. I am dying of internal thirst. I need water in all the places where my soul has gone to sleep. The water would wake me. This is both literal and figurative. It is figurative in the ways I have mentioned. It is literal in that the anti-psychotics are fucking with my mouth in very bad and uncomfortable ways. Do you understand?

LIDDY: I think so. Could I bring you some water?

STEPHEN: That would be nice.

liddy brings water

(LIDDY *brings water.*)

LIDDY: I brought Crystal Geyser. Is Crystal Geyser okay? Or do you like Spa better?

STEPHEN: Crystal Geyser is fine. Thank you.

LIDDY: You've been sleeping a lot.

STEPHEN: I'm tired. (*Changing the subject*) Why are you named Liddy? Are you named after someone?

LIDDY: Alice.

STEPHEN: Alice who?

LIDDY: Alice in Wonderland.

STEPHEN: But your name isn't Alice; it's Liddy.

LIDDY: My mother was original. She wanted to name me after Alice Liddell, the little girl that Lewis Carroll wrote the story for, only Mom thought that Alice was too common, so she called me Liddell. But nobody calls me Liddell—just Liddy. And you? Who are you named for?

STEPHEN: I never asked. Probably the saint. My parents were unoriginal. My brother is named Peter.

LIDDY: Mine is Emerson; like the philosopher. He goes by Em. Are you and your brother close?

STEPHEN: No. We're rather un-close. You know, your name is appropriate. It fits. You're a bit like Alice—in Wonderland—with the crazy people.

LIDDY: You know, it's dangerous to label your own experience as "crazy".

STEPHEN: You don't think I'm crazy?

LIDDY: No. I don't know what that means anyway.

STEPHEN: You're in denial.

LIDDY: Probably.

STEPHEN: The paranormal is a great place to visit, but I don't want to live here permanantly.

LIDDY: What constitutes paranormal?

STEPHEN: Well, this.

LIDDY: This situation? This hospital? Or the events that you led you to this hospital?

STEPHEN: All of the above.

LIDDY: Lets talk about that.

STEPHEN: You like your job.

LIDDY: Yes.

STEPHEN: What do you like about your job?

LIDDY: I like people. Their stories.

STEPHEN: That's nice.

LIDDY: Are you being facetious?

STEPHEN: As opposed to figurative?

LIDDY: As opposed to sincere.

STEPHEN: Probably.

LIDDY: How can I help you? What do you want from me in this siuation?

STEPHEN: I don't think I want anything.

LIDDY: Okay. So how can I help you?

STEPHEN: You already asked that.

LIDDY: Did you answer?

STEPHEN: No.

LIDDY: I don't think you're "crazy".

STEPHEN: Today the doctor said I'm not manic depressive and I'm not bipolar and I'm not schizophrenic, but he doesn't know what's wrong with me. In other words, he doesn't know what I am. And he changed my prescription again.

LIDDY: What if you're just having a breakdown? I mean, what if you're not any of those things, and you're just you and you're having a breakdown?

STEPHEN: I appreciate what you're tying to do, but don't.

LIDDY: Don't what?

STEPHEN: Don't make me feel better.

LIDDY: I'm not making you feel better.

STEPHEN: Exactly. Don't make friends with crazy people, Liddy Green. It's unprofessional and also bad for you.

LIDDY: I'll remember that. Thanks.

(Lights up on EMERSON, *alone.)*

EMERSON: I don't worry about people. I think it's selfish. Worrying. It's usually about the person worrying and not the object of the worry. But I worry about my sister. She's my sister. Which means she's enough like me that I worry. And she's impetuous. I try to keep an eye on her. I visit. I visit her more than she visits me. I'm older, and I think this means that it's my job to visit more. I look out for her. At least I try. Sometimes she makes that challenging.

liddy consults her brother

LIDDY: I see light all around him.

EMERSON: Like an aura?

LIDDY: I've never seen an aura before. I just see this light. Like a cloud. And his face sort of melts into the cloud, he gets very near and then very far. It's weird, Em. It's so wrong. It's unprofessional. But, you know, I don't really buy any of that professionalism bullshit anyway. I mean, why does professionalism always have to be about distance?

EMERSON: Because you're in the mental health field, and there's this thing about not getting involved. It's like a rule.

LIDDY: I know. I'm breaking rules.

EMERSON: What are you doing with him?

LIDDY: What do you mean?

EMERSON: What do you hope to get from this man?

LIDDY: He needs love.

EMERSON: And what do you need?

LIDDY: I would open his mouth and pour light inside of him, fill every pour with light, like oil, like I were pouring oil into an engine. I would set his room on fire with light, float the furniture two feet off the ground and leave it all suspended in the air that he might awaken to radiance and heal himself.

EMERSON: You're starting to sound sort of crazy yourself.

LIDDY: It's in the blood, Honey. Remember Mom? It is in our fucking blood.

EMERSON: Great.

LIDDY: I want you to meet him.

EMERSON: No.

LIDDY: Please? All that stuff he talks about, I don't think he's crazy. I just think he's—

EMERSON: Experiencing the doubt, uncertainty and base suffering of the human experience?

LIDDY: Yes. Something like that.

EMERSON: No.

(LIDDY *pouts. She knows that this works.*)

EMERSON: No. You want me to visit the crazy guy.

LIDDY: Don't call him the crazy guy.

EMERSON: The suffering guy.

LIDDY: Fine.

EMERSON: You want me to visit him – because you think he's a visionary?

LIDDY: Because maybe it'll help.

liddy brings more water

LIDDY: I brought water. Evian. Did you know Evian is naive spelled backwards?

STEPHEN: I didn't know that. I'm doing grape flavored ginger ale these days. But, thanks.

LIDDY: You eat garbage. Do you know there are studies that link depression to sugar consumption?

STEPHEN: Your point?

LIDDY: I don't have one. Want to meet my brother?

STEPHEN: How did you manage that? Getting your brother a visitors' pass? Awfully special, aren't you?

LIDDY: Yes. Awfully. I asked for one and got it. So, do you want to meet him? He's a Buddhist.

STEPHEN: Oh, great. We can be empty rice bowls together. Listen, I'm tired. Group really wears me out. And last night we had a talent show. It was draining. It takes a lot out of me to be on stage. We performers need our rest. And our chocolate milkshakes and our donuts and our M & Ms, for that matter. It's a life. A whole life thing. And, you know, what better place to consume sugar that will make you depressed than the Psych Ward where you can get *lots* of drugs to fix it all? You know what I mean there, Miss Social Worker?

LIDDY: My brother is going to be at the hospital tomorrow morning. If you like, you can meet him. If not, you can fake being comatose and avoid him.

STEPHEN: Comatose?

LIDDY: I'm joking.

STEPHEN: I know.

emerson does not bring water.

EMERSON: Excuse me, may I come in?

STEPHEN: I don't know. Who are you?

EMERSON: I'm Emerson Green. Liddy's brother. *(Silence)* I'm visiting from the Pacific Northwest. *(Silence)* Liddy says you're a poet.

(STEPHEN shrugs.)

EMERSON: I wrote poetry once. When I was fifteen and in love with the girl who sat in front of me in Algebra. I wrote algebra poems. A series of them while I copied equations off the board and studied the back of her head.

STEPHEN: Every hair, right? For me it was Political Science. Algebra was too engrossing for crushes.

EMERSON: Can we talk about you?

STEPHEN: I do a lot of that these days. Are you a trained clinician? That's not a word is it? I mean someone who is trained clinically. I don't mean "psychologist" exactly. But, clinically trained.

EMERSON: I'm not clinically trained. I'm just a Western Buddhist and a math teacher. I guess I'm trained to teach math. But my sister has taken rather an unusual liking to you, and she and I are very close.

STEPHEN: I've heard. Have you read James Joyce? Because my father keeps sending me *The Portrait of the Artist as a Young Man* and I have about twelve copies by now. Would you like one?

EMERSON: Um, no thank you. I read Joyce in college, and to be honest, I didn't get too much out of it. You know? I'm a math guy, I guess. I like things with answers. And formulas.

STEPHEN: Literature doesn't have answers.

EMERSON: I know.

STEPHEN: It's all subjective.

EMERSON: Right. *(Beat)* Liddy says you admitted yourself here. Do you have plans to leave?

STEPHEN: *(Shrugs)* Not in my hands.

EMERSON: Of course it's in your hands. You're pretty smart—you know that.

STEPHEN: Okay.

EMERSON: Do you have therapy?

STEPHEN: We have this group. I hate the group. I'm anti-social in the group. The other day, someone accused me of being passive-aggressive in the group. But, mostly, we have medication. They do a lot with medication. They change mine frequently. And, we have your sister. And each other. And I have James Joyce. James Joyce helps a lot.

EMERSON: Liddy thinks that you're very smart.

STEPHEN: I'm really just very tired.

EMERSON: Of course. I'm sorry for bothering you.

STEPHEN: No bother. Really. Come back another day. Emerson, right? But they call you Em. Liddy says you are close.

EMERSON: It was nice to meet you.

liddy recounts a dream, or "i wouldn't have locked her up"

LIDDY: I dreamed about Mom last night. Mom was driving a car - which we all tried to get her not to do when she was alive - and I was in the passenger seat. We drove past Grandma's house and kept going. We looked out the window at the red and purple tulips in

Grandma's front yard. And Mom said, "This is where it happened. "

Where what happened?

And she said, "There are things you don't know." We are driving on the water. The car floats like a raft, and Mom keeps saying, "There are secrets and you don't know them. "

And I want her to tell me the secrets, but she disappears and I am left there on top of the water alone. But I want to know the secrets.

EMERSON: What do you think it means?

LIDDY: Don't go driving with crazy people.

EMERSON: He seems very nice.

LIDDY: Nice? I wouldn't say "nice".

EMERSON: Well, I have no idea if he's crazy. I don't really know what that means anyway.

LIDDY: I know.

EMERSON: I thought Mom was kind of okay.

(LIDDY *reacts maybe?*)

EMERSON: I mean, until she wasn't.

LIDDY: I really like him. I know I'm not supposed to, but I do. I really do. If he weren't in a hospital...who knows?

EMERSON: You know you have to leave him alone, right?

LIDDY: I don't think he's crazy.

EMERSON: I don't think that's the issue.

LIDDY: I want to take care of him. I want to give him my body to feed off of—my arms for strength, my legs for motion, my breasts for his hunger. I want to hold him captive—kidnap him and take him to the mountains and make him well again. Pour water into the places where he is dry.

EMERSON: You're making him sound like a houseplant.

LIDDY: You don't get it.

EMERSON: I'm trying to help. Look. Honey. Don't fall in love with someone in the hospital. Not only is that shitting where you proverbially eat, but it is also not a strong character choice. It does not speak well for the potential of a relationship when one of the partners is not free to come and go without a pass.

LIDDY: What if we broke him out? Kidnapped him and escaped to Seattle and set up house together, all three of us?

EMERSON: Okay, number one, *No*. Number two, I don't want to set up house with a mad poet. I'm not the one engaging in obsession—you are, so you can set up your house without me. Number three, absolutely no, because it's really the most irrational and stupid and childish thing you're said since you were fourteen and you wanted to sell Mom. You have to leave him alone. His path is his own.

LIDDY: I know. I mean, of course I know that.

EMERSON: Of course you do.

LIDDY: Of course.

EMERSON: Wonderful.

LIDDY: But I think about him.

EMERSON: Think about him how?

LIDDY: I am drawn to him.

EMERSON: That doesn't sound good.

LIDDY: He knows the things Mom knew.

EMERSON: I don't think those are good things.

LIDDY: It doesn't matter. I want to know those things too. And maybe I am drawn to him for a good reason. A good one. Maybe it's all going to work out. Maybe I could love him. And maybe that is exactly what he needs. And maybe that's what I need to. We could reverse all the laws.

EMERSON: No. This is exactly the thing. Don't reverse the laws, Liddy. I can't talk to you if you're going to—

LIDDY: If I'm going to what? *(No answer)* If I'm going to what?

EMERSON: Do you have some sort of counselor or shrink at the hospital that you could talk to?

LIDDY: Sure. *(Beat)* Okay, what if this were a part of something bigger than mental health? A plan. For our lives.

EMERSON: There is nothing besides the moment to moment truth of the breath, of observation, of witnessing impersonal passing phenomenon.

LIDDY: Whatever. I mean something else altogether.

EMERSON: Like what!?

LIDDY: Like destiny.

EMERSON: That scares me, Lid.

LIDDY: Destiny?

EMERSON: You.

LIDDY: Really?

liddy crosses the line

LIDDY: I need to tell you things.

STEPHEN: Like what?

LIDDY: Like, I am drawn to you.

STEPHEN: Really?

LIDDY: Yes. I see lights emanating from your head and body; I believe this is your aura.

STEPHEN: That's weird.

LIDDY: Sure. But I'm seeing these things.

STEPHEN: Are we on the same medication? You're freaking me out.

LIDDY: I am freaking myself out. But I'm not afraid of that. Of freaking myself out. Of the paranormal. Of anything. I see a meadow, and you are in the meadow and you are holding hands with a girl, and it's me, the girl is me, and it is all part of a big plan to stop the world's pain or reroute it or bring it out of the closet and it's connected to my mother and the secrets she knew and I'm thinking crazy things—I'm driving on the surface of water and thinking—

STEPHEN: Yes. You are—

LIDDY: —I'm thinking about breaking you out of the hospital and taking you to Seattle.

STEPHEN: Why Seattle?

LIDDY: I don't know. The music scene. My brother. I don't know. What do you think of this?

STEPHEN: Of what?

LIDDY: Of any of it. Me. What do you think of me?

(Beat)

STEPHEN: I can't.

LIDDY: I know—

STEPHEN: I just...I like when you come to see me. But I can't feel anything right now. So I don't.

LIDDY: I do.

STEPHEN: Don't.

LIDDY: But I do.

STEPHEN: I'm sorry.

LIDDY: I want to touch you.

STEPHEN: You do?

(LIDDY nods.)

STEPHEN: Why?

LIDDY: I don't know why. Because I do.

STEPHEN: Don't.

(And now we see EMERSON again, speaking to us.)

EMERSON: I try to look out for her. She's enough
like me, but enough like the other parts of the
family that aren't like me—impetuous, impulsive—
impressionable—

*(LIDDY reaches her hand out to touch STEPHEN. It is not a
sexual touch, per se. She may just reach out and barely touch
his cheek or even his hand. There is a dread in the touch and
perhaps something sensual—but it is the desire to make
contact.)*

*(STEPHEN pulls away at the last minute and LIDDY pulls her
hand back, realizing she has indeed crossed a line, and that
this is totally and wholly wrong.)*

STEPHEN: Please don't.

LIDDY: You're right. I'm sorry. I'm so so sorry. *(She
leaves abruptly.)*

STEPHEN: Well, you don't have to go.

liddy consults a professional

LIDDY: I got attached to someone on the ward. I grew fond of him. I spent more time than I should have. I brought him bottled water every day. I started to think that I was this angel sent to bring him spring water because he was dry. He was a poet. He went to a fancy school and used fancy words and referenced Joyce and and he was funny. He made me laugh. My mom was sort of crazy. Maybe that's it. Maybe he was familiar. I mean, all the psychiatrists would say that, right? And all the kings horses and all the kings men couldn't put Liddy together again—Freud, Jung, Alice Miller, all of 12 Steps, the whole mental health thing. I'm thinking maybe I need a new job. Maybe a new field. Maybe a new place to live, too.
What do you think?

SOCIAL WORKER: Why do you think you're here?

LIDDY: I'm feeling overwhelmed.

SOCIAL WORKER: What, in particular, is overwhelming you?

LIDDY: The world's pain. Have you ever felt that?

SOCIAL WORKER: Not really. No, I can't say that I have.

LIDDY: I think it's getting to be a lot more common, you know. I think one day we will all wake up to feel overwhelmed. A great big awakening of overwhelm ed-ness and maybe terror. A great big disillusioning light bringing wave.

SOCIAL WORKER: Is there anything I can do for you? Anything you need?

LIDDY: No, thank you. I'll be just fine.

END OF PART ONE

part two

winter with tambourine boy

(LIDDY *tells us a story.*)

LIDDY: It is Janurary, and I am nineteen, home from my first semester at school.

You are my friend from home. This is home, and you are my friend. And since my mother died, there is no one to stay with anymore, when I come home. So, I come home to you—with your big steel-tipped boots and your pierced ear and your apartment on Armitage Street, next to the El tracks.

I am here, and you are not.

You are in Indiana shooting a drivers' ed training film. We call that "an industrial," we in the know. You have the lead in this industrial, which is funny since you don't know how to drive, but you're faking it ok for the cameras.

Now, the light in your apartment affects me in funny ways. It makes me dance around the kitchen in thermal underwear or lie on the floor under patches of sun, hoping to soak the fragmented sunlight into my skin because Chicago in January can be cruel. The light makes me color with my red and purple crayons on your lime green linoleum floor. Just for effect. The light makes me eat things I normally wouldn't eat, like chocolate milk and toast, because that's all you've got here, and for some reason I'm just too lame to go buy anything else. The light makes me steal toilet paper from the diner around the corner because you never buy any, and it makes me put the rolls of stolen toilet paper in your big Guatemalen bag and buy a cup of coffee and run. The light is making me do all of these things; it's one of those real dizzy intoxicating lights, like the light that shines off your skin and teeth and hair. And you aren't even here so this is in my memory.

You call and leave messages for me to listen to on the machine. You call every day from that motel in Indiana.

The messages go like this:

BEEP

I say, Hey, it's me, and I'm in your apartment.

And, you say, "Make yourself at home."

And I say, Okay. I'm gonna go out this afternoon in the fucking freezing cold, maybe to the art museum. When are you coming home? It's cold here. And what's up with your heat?

And you say, " Use the space heater in the bedroom. It's really awesome and it's the only way to get warm at all. "

And I say, the space heater rocks my world.

And you say, "Good."

The night you come home, (At last!!) you entertain me with stories about the cast and crew and the director who kept trying to get you to "ground." Neither of us knows what that means - "to ground." We conjecture, but we really don't know. I am on the floor again - or still - in your room this time, pressed up against the heater. Which you were right about. With my legs shooting straight in the air, my skirt down around my ears, long johns exposed.

You come home, bringing trail mix and cheap ice cream and we eat it for dinner and tell stories of our days apart.

You brought your tambourine with you to Indiana ("Maybe that's why she thought you were ungrounded," I say) and you brought it home again. So after eating all the ice cream, we pretend to be a tambourine band on the streets of your North Side neighborhood. This lasts as long as the wind chill permits, which is actually sort of long.

Now, I have gotten very good at giving out this address as my own. Do you even know how many people I give your address to? Phone number, maybe, because I know they call. But address. Sometimes even your last name. I pretend that it is mine, I don't know why, really.

A week passes. Just like this. And then a second. You're in school now - while I'm on vacation - and I hang out around the theater building watching all the actors who you assure me will one day be famous. We take bets on which ones. And I drink lemon tea all afternoon at Java Jive and mocha lattes at Kava Kave. And I wait for you to get done and we make drama.

"Lets pretend we're married," you say, like the Prince song—it is a song—and so we do. I wear a tin foil ring for a whole three days until it falls off.

One night, late, we take a walk West, over the bridge to a cafe called Voltaire, and on the way we meet an old lady who talks to us in Spanish and puts her hand on my belly as if I am pregnant. I am certainly not pregnant, since we have never had sex, never even kissed on the mouth, although I think of both of these as valid options but just don't tell you and I don't' know how to seduce. So, unless it is a virgin birth, I cannot be pregnant, though I think I would like to be—with myself. I would like to give birth. And I wonder if now, after her touch on my flat virgin belly, I will.

I am going back to California soon. Berkeley. That's where I go to school. And between you and me, I don't know if that is really a good idea. My brother is nearby, and I see him a lot. But Berkeley is a weird place to be if you're a nineteen year old girl with a dead crazy mom and a Buddhist brother and a heart somewhere else.

But for now, I'm still in Chicago with you. I'm in your blue painted shower singing songs and using your towels. I'm on your green chair eating Cheerios and chocolate milk. I'm hopping up and down on one leg and listening to all of your favorite songs from the nineteen-eighties because it is now the end of the decade and we feel we should take stock.

A month later, Valentines Day—but that is just a coincidence—you call me at school, telling me to watch for you on some TV fast food commercial, and so I do. You are the same. I am the same. We are too young to know anything really about how friendship changes or how we'll lose one another. Both of which will be unavoidable. But we do not know about that. We are still best friends. You were the one I called. That day. Before I called Em. I called you. Do you remember?

END OF PART TWO

part three
self reliance

EMERSON: My mother killed herself during Finals in the Spring of my sophomore year at Stanford. I was working on an independent study for Eastern philosophy, failing Romantic Lit, dating a girl called Susan, oh and I had recently begun to meditate. My sister called to tell me our mother had died.

LIDDY: Em?

EMERSON: She was a senior in high school, with two months to go before graduation. It was eerie how calm she sounded. Efficient. Clinical. Detached.

(EMERSON *turns to* LIDDY *and they enter scene, the phone call.)*

EMERSON: Why do you sound like that?

LIDDY: Like what? I don't.

EMERSON: You do.

LIDDY: I don't know. There's a lot to do.

EMERSON: Well, it's wrong.

LIDDY: What do you want me to do? Kill myself? I mean, fall apart?

EMERSON: Maybe.

LIDDY: I'm fine.

EMERSON: You're not fine.

LIDDY: Yes, I am.

EMERSON: Fine. Be fine.

LIDDY: Fine. *(Beat)* When are you coming home?

EMERSON: Who are you staying with?

LIDDY: Julia.

EMERSON: Who's that?

LIDDY: My friend. You don't know her.

EMERSON: I don't know her.

LIDDY: I'm staying with her.

EMERSON: I'll be back for the funeral. I guess I'll get on a plane tomorrow? This is all happening very fast.

LIDDY: It's tomorrow.

EMERSON: Tomorrow. I'll get on a plane.

LIDDY: Yes. Do you have to go right back?

EMERSON: I don't know. I guess I do. I have finals. Did you cry?

LIDDY: I don't know. What time will you come in?

EMERSON: How the Hell should I know? I'm talking to you, not the travel agent.

LIDDY: Right.

EMERSON: Sorry. I don't know when I'm coming. I'll call you back.

LIDDY: Okay.

EMERSON: I love you.

LIDDY: I love you too.

EMERSON: Wait. How did she—?

LIDDY: Pills.

(EMERSON *digests this.*)

LIDDY: Washed down by diet soda. *(Beat)* I guess she didn't want to gain any weight in case it didn't work.

EMERSON: That sounds like Mom.

LIDDY: She left flowers all over the room. No note. I guess it was suicide. I mean, you can't take that many pills by accident. Or drop that many flowers.

EMERSON: She could have. The pills, I mean.

LIDDY: Yeah. They were yellow. The flowers, not the pills. I couldn't do anything for a really long time. I mean, it took me such a long time before I could call anybody. The ambulence. The—I don't know. She was really happy all week. Luminous. Happy.

EMERSON: Shouldn't I have known? Why didn't I know?

LIDDY: I didn't know.

EMERSON: She was our mother. We should have known.

LIDDY: But we didn't. She was really happy. Maybe I did. But I didn't. She changed when you went to school. I mean, she was always emotional, but it was different. Unless she had always been like that and I didn't notice. She couldn't stop crying. And she had these moodswings, really extreme ones. She thought everyone was out to get her and she wouldn't stop talking about the end of the world. I don't know. I should have done something, but I didn't know what to do. Besides no one believes you when you say your mom is crazy. They just think you're having some kind of teenage problem.

EMERSON: Our mother was just a person living out her destiny.

LIDDY: A destiny of diet soda and yellow flowers.

EMERSON: Yes.

LIDDY: Well, I'll see you tomorrow.

EMERSON: I love you.

LIDDY: Me too. I'll see you tomorrow. Take a cab, okay?

EMERSON: Okay. I'll have to call you back anyway, once I know when. Okay?

LIDDY: I bet it'll be cheaper if you tell the airlines your mom died. Maybe really cheap if you actually say the world "suicide".

EMERSON: Yeah. I'll get the tragedy discount.

LIDDY: I think it's called the Bereavement Fare.

EMERSON: And then I have to come back for finals.

LIDDY: Okay.

EMERSON: And we'll figure it all out. I mean, about you and me. About what, what we'll do now. We have cousins somewhere, don't we? Didn't we used to have cousins?

LIDDY: I don't know. I guess we have cousins. That fat girl in Ohio. And the...aren't there cousins from...where are they?

EMERSON: I don't know.

LIDDY: I don't think we kept in touch with cousins.

EMERSON: Go through Mom's phone book. Just call people.

LIDDY: Okay.

EMERSON: You call half, and I'll call the other half once I get there. Or, you know what, just call who you want.

LIDDY: Tomorrow.

EMERSON: Right. Tomorrow. I'll be there.

LIDDY: Okay.

EMERSON: Okay. *(To audience)* I went there. There was a funeral. It was outside. I came back to school. I started to get ready for Finals. I had nightmares. I had them a lot.

em has a bad dream

(EMERSON *is in bed with* SUSAN, *a young woman in her early 20s. It is his sophomore year at Stanford, the suicide still very new. He has a nightmare. Wakes up startled or suddenly, as if he were going to arrive home in time to save* MOM *but doesn't make it in time. His first lines may be said either in the nightmare, or after, upon waking.*)

EMERSON: Mom?

SUSAN: What, Honey? What is it?

EMERSON: Oh.

SUSAN: Yeah?

EMERSON: You know.

SUSAN: Yeah. Again?

EMERSON: Yeah, again.

SUSAN: Well it's recent. It's really recent.

EMERSON: Yeah.

SUSAN: It takes years, Em. It does.

EMERSON: Yeah.

SUSAN: Oh, Honey—

(SUSAN *holds* EMERSON, *he settles into her embrace.*)

EMERSON: Sus?

SUSAN: Yeah?

EMERSON: Why'd she ..?

SUSAN: I don't know.

EMERSON: Sus?

SUSAN: Yeah?

EMERSON: I'm going to fail Romantic Lit. And I want my mom.

SUSAN: I know, Sweetheart.

EMERSON: I want my mother.

(SUSAN *holds* EMERSON.)

long distance

EMERSON: Is anyone holding you?

LIDDY: Sure.

EMERSON: Who? Who's holding you?

LIDDY: Well, lots of people. Why? Why is it so important that I'm held?

EMERSON: I have Susan. It helps. She thinks that someone needs to hold you, and I would hold you, only I won't be back until you graduate, and I know I held you at the funeral, but is someone holding you now? We're just looking out for you. We love you.

LIDDY: I'm fine, Em. Really. You can hold me all you want once you get here. But right now I really just want to finish high school and pack the house up and donate Mom's things to the appropriate places. Do you have any preference over Goodwill versus Salvation Army versus...I don't know...B'nai Brith?

EMERSON: No. It's all the same to me. Hey, Lid, you know anything about Buddhism?

LIDDY: A little.

EMERSON: Do you think we exist?

LIDDY: Definitely. I know I do. Mom doesn't anymore. But I do.

EMERSON: Do you ever watch your breath?

LIDDY: No. I think I'm going to give her things to B'nai Brith. Keep it in the tribe, you know?

EMERSON: What tribe?

LIDDY: The Jews.

EMERSON: Oh. I kind of feel like I'm becoming a Buddhist these days. But we'll see.

LIDDY: Em? I have a crush on the school psychologist. He's thirty, and we have a lot in common.

EMERSON: Really? Observe it, Lid. Don't act on the crush, just observe the sensations.

LIDDY: I don't think I'd be a very good Buddhist. I'm kind of into action.

EMERSON: Don't do anything til I get there.

LIDDY: That may be too late.

liddy and the school psychologist

ROBERT: It isn't your fault. You couldn't have done anything. Your mother was acting out her own desperation. You couldn't have saved her.

LIDDY: Everyone says that to me. Everyone says that.

ROBERT: It's true. Everyone says that because it's true.

LIDDY: But what does it mean? What does it mean to "save" her? I just...never mind.

ROBERT: Do you miss her?

LIDDY: Yeah.

ROBERT: Tell me about your mom. Tell me what you loved about her.

LIDDY: She took me to the ballet. And sometimes on these weird field trips. Like one day, she took me on this completely made-up trip to look at houses, even though we weren't moving. She just wanted to look at them. And she pretended to the real estate agent that we wanted to put in a pool. I don't know why she did that. But it was fun. And then we got cupcakes afterwards. That was fun, too.

ROBERT: Sounds fun.

LIDDY: She let me miss school for that.

ROBERT: Sounds fun.

LIDDY: Have you read *Tender is the Night*? We're reading it in Honors English, and there's this woman in the book, Nicole, and she's insane and also very beautiful and everyone falls in love with her and she's the best person in the story. See, I want to be the best person in the story. Only I can't because my mother is the best person in the story. Only I need her to be my mother, not Nicole Diver.

I could make her stop crying, you know. I yelled at her. That's how. I'd just yell. I'd be like, "Mom, stop it. Right now!" And she would. I mean, she'd fight with me, but she'd get out of bed.

ROBERT: You weren't repsonsible.

LIDDY: Have you read *Tender is the Night*?

ROBERT: Sure. Years ago. I loved it. It's a better work, I think, than *Gatsby*. You know, Nicole is based on Scott Fitzgerard's wife, Zelda. She burned down buildings and danced on table tops. Ended up hospitalized. Your mother was out of control. I don't know if anyone could have done anything. I'm... I'm sorry that we didn't know the extent of anything here at school.

LIDDY: You couldn't have done anything anyway. So Zelda burned down buildings? I would like to do something like that some time. I never get to do anything damaging.

ROBERT: Do something damaging right now.

LIDDY: Like what?

ROBERT: Say something you think you can't say.

LIDDY: I have a crush on you.

ROBERT: Good! What?

LIDDY: I have a crush on you. I think we have a lot in common. I think about...you know. Oh, now I feel really stupid.

ROBERT: I'm flattered. I don't know what to say besides that.

LIDDY: That's okay. You don't have to say anything.

ROBERT: Can I buy you an ice cream cone or something?

emerson tries to detach

EMERSON: My sister has a crush on her school psychologist. Can he be arrested for that?

SUSAN: Only if they have sex. Are they having sex?

EMERSON: No. She just said she had a crush. She did not use the word sex. FUCK! I have to go home. Fuck Romantic Lit. Fuck Eastern philosophy. Fuck Stanford. I have to go home and make sure my sister is not having sex before she turns eighteen, for Christsakes.

SUSAN: Honey, you're over reacting. I had sex when I was eighteen.

EMERSON: Yeah, but...this is my little sister!

SUSAN: Thanks alot.

EMERSON: And who is this Robert guy anyway? Doesn't he know better?

SUSAN: You said she didn't say sex. Right? Maybe nothing is happening. Maybe it's just a crush like you said.

EMERSON: It had better be just a crush. This man had better have some kind of moral boundaries or whatever. Jesus.

SUSAN: Ethical boundaries.

EMERSON: What!?

SUSAN: You're talking about ethics, not morals.

EMERSON: What!? I'm sorry. I'm sorry. Shit. I'm sorry. Okay, wait. I can observe this. Wait. I have to watch this sensation.

SUSAN: What are you talking about?

EMERSON: Buddhism! Aren't you following this? I'm hungry. Have you noticed that nothing stays open past ten in California? Is it a state law or something?

SUSAN: Do you think she'll want to stay the summer here at Stanford? We could get her a job. She shouldn't be alone.

EMERSON: No one should be alone. What if I can't sleep again?

SUSAN: I don't know. Read?

EMERSON: Why are there no all night diners in California?

SUSAN: You could go the City.

EMERSON: I hate the City. I want to sleep.

SUSAN: Em, you're grieving. It's just grief.

EMERSON: (Lashing out) Get off my case, okay? I have enough to deal with without you telling me I'm grieving. How the fuck would you know? Do you know what this feels like?

SUSAN: I'm sorry. I don't. I have no idea what this feels like. I' m sorry.

EMERSON: You're damn right you have no idea. You have your little perfect family out there in Mill Fucking Valley. It sounds like a cereal company. You have a perfect life, a perfect grade point average, money, a mother who makes holiday dinners and a family who takes trips together. You don't know a thing. You have no complaints.

SUSAN: I'm going to the library now. When I come home, you had better be ready to apologize.

EMERSON: The Buddha said that suffering exists. That was the contribution he made to the philosophical debate of the time. He said it wasn't just illusion, it was real, but that we could transcend it through careful observation. Detachment.

SUSAN: What the fuck are you talking about? I don't think you're supposed to be detached when your mom kills herself.

EMERSON: Oh you think?

SUSAN: I'm trying to help.

EMERSON: Well, don't. Don't try to help me. You worry about you, and I'll worry about me.

long distance (again)

LIDDY: I'd have been pissed if you talked to me like that.

EMERSON: What do you know about it?

LIDDY: She was probably trying to help.

EMERSON: Yeah, probably. I'm very reactive.

LIDDY: Whatever that means.

EMERSON: You fuck your school psychologist yet?

LIDDY: Will you stop it? I'm not doing anything like that. It isn't like that, okay? He takes me out for ice cream. We've had ice cream three times this week. I always get vanilla. I think he feels bad about Mom.

EMERSON: As long as it's just ice cream.

LIDDY: Will you quit it?

EMERSON: Why are you so well adjusted?

LIDDY: I don't know. I'm not well adjusted.

EMERSON: Could have fooled me. You sound well adjusted. I'm angry all the time. Are you?

LIDDY: No. I'm not really sure what I am. I feel different than other people. I just feel...I don't know. Like the kids in the books where they go off and...we're orphans now, you know.

EMERSON: We're not orphans. We have a father.

LIDDY: We're orphans.

EMERSON: Yeah. You want to spend your summer out here in Palo Alto? Why don't you come out here? We'll get you settled here with me and Susan. We're not orphans, Liddy. We have each other.

LIDDY: I'd love to come out there. I think I'm going to take a year off before college. Could I do that where you are?

EMERSON: Yes. It's very common out here. Time off. This whole area is filled with people taking time off.

LIDDY: Do you ever think about Mom?

EMERSON: Sure

LIDDY: What do you think? When you think about her?

EMERSON: (Shrugs) I think about...her taste in clothes. She liked yellow.

LIDDY: A lot.

EMERSON: I think about how she used to read us stories. Remember?

LIDDY: Yeah.

EMERSON: Everyone tells me she's in a better place.

LIDDY: I guess.

EMERSON: I don't really believe in that, though. I don't believe in "place." Not after you die.

LIDDY: I miss her.

EMERSON: I'm coming out there to see you graduate.

LIDDY: Next week.

EMERSON: Next week. And I'm bringing you back with me. You can spend your year off here.

LIDDY: Okay.

EMERSON: And don't you dare touch this psychologist guy. I will personally see that his ass gets fired if you do. You're a minor. Even if you don't act like one.

LIDDY: Apologize to you girlfriend, will you? And don't tell me what to do.

EMERSON: I'll be there next week. Okay?

LIDDY: I'm glad. I'm glad you're coming home.

emerson watches his breath

(EMERSONgoes to meditation practice. CARLA is his teacher.)

CARLA: You see therapy is not important. Not necessary. What's therapy? Therapy just reinforces the idea that you exist, that anything the mind says or does is real. What is important is that you watch the breath. Just watch. To observe and not be involved, yes, that is the secret. The wonder. To watch.

EMERSON: The breath.

CARLA: Yes. Start by observing the breath as it passes over the space just below the nostrils. If you confine your awareness to a very tiny space, it will be easier to understand, to watch.

EMERSON: To observe.

CARLA: Yes. The breath. Through the nostrils. Not the mouth. The nostrils.

(EMERSON *watches his breath.*)

EMERSON: Can I learn to observe nightmares?

CARLA: Of course you can. What sort of nightmares?

EMERSON: Well, my mother killed herself recently and I have nightmares in which I am trying to find her so that she won't die. Can I learn to observe this as meaningless sensation? My mother took a lot of sleeping pills and now she can sleep, and I can't. I don't sleep. I wish that I could.

So my question for you is, can this be observed? Can it all be passing, impersonal phenomon?

Can this grief be witnessed but not identified with?

CARLA: Yes. In time, with practice, yes. But therapy might not be a bad idea. Therapy could prove to be quite useful.

I'm sorry about your mother. Is there anything I can do to help?

EMERSON: I don't think so. But thank you for asking.

therapy could prove quite useful

(EMERSON *comes home.* SUSAN *is packing.*)

EMERSON: Where are you going?

SUSAN: On a perfect trip with my perfect family. We're spending the perfect weekend perfectly camping in Big Sur. Do you want to come?

EMERSON: I'm sorry I said all that. About, you know. I just...I'm sorry.

SUSAN: I know you are.

EMERSON: Don't go?

SUSAN: Come with us.

EMERSON: How can I?

SUSAN: Just come. We want you. I want you. We'll only be gone two days.

EMERSON: Two days?

SUSAN: Maybe you'll sleep better at Big Sur. It's really beautiful.

EMERSON: Yeah? Is it okay? I mean, am I allowed to go to Big Sur? Shouldn't I be staying home and grieving or something?

SUSAN: I think you're allowed to go to Big Sur. *(Beat)* It'll take time, Honey. It just might take a while.

EMERSON: I don't believe in time.

SUSAN: Okay.

(SUSAN *kisses* EMERSON.)

EMERSON: You're a wonderful person.

SUSAN: Whenever a man says that to me, it always makes me think he's leaving. It sounds so unromantic.

EMERSON: You're a wonderful person. And I'm not leaving. I want to go with your family to Big Sur.

SUSAN: Good. I already told them you would.

EMERSON: You're---

SUSAN: I'm the best.

EMERSON: I'm going to therapy.

SUSAN: Good. I think it will help.

EMERSON: I do, too.

goodnight moon

(EMERSON *is meditating.* MOM *appears, as if in a vision, wearing yellow. She is played by the actress playing* LIDDY. *This should be very magical.*)

MOM: Em?

EMERSON: Go away. I'm meditating.

MOM: You're having a vision, Honey.

EMERSON: Mom?

MOM: That's right. Surprise. Death is incredible, Em. Everything is stripped away. No stretch marks, no scar tissue, no pain. It is remarkable. An adventure. I raised you kids to have adventures, and goddammit, you're going to have them. Don't let this mess up the journey. I'm fine. I'm doing what I wanted to do.
Oh, by the way, I'm going to be reincarnated in Iowa as a little girl called Alice and discover a non-pharmaceutical cure for schizophrenia. Isn't that great? Big Sur is amazing, huh? I was there once before you kids were born. I thought it was the most beautiful place on Earth.

EMERSON: Are you going to visit Liddy too?

MOM: No. I can't do this too often, it's draining. Dead people really just need to stay dead. It takes a lot out of us when we have to be apparations.

Now, personally, I think this meditation thing is for shit. But don't listen to me. I wasn't very happy, was I?

EMERSON: Why are you here?

MOM: I'm trying to tell you how incredible it is to be dead. I have all sorts of powers I didn't have when I was alive. Like clarity. I've found clarity. And complete dissolution. I've dissolved.

EMERSON: That could be liberating.

MOM: And I want to tell you that I love you. Never doubt that. You and your sister were the light of my life and I loved you tremendously. Fiercely.

EMERSON: Is this really a vision?

MOM: No, Honey. You're just sleeping. You're asleep. Isn't it nice? You missed sleep, didn't you? No more nightmares, okay? No more of that. You just sleep through the night, just like when you were a little boy. I'll hold you and you'll sleep, and only good things can happen while you sleep.
Goodnight, Moon. Goodnight faces everywhere. No, that's not it. Not faces. What did we say goodnight to? You remember that book, don't you?

EMERSON: Sure. Goodnight Moon.

MOM: Goodnight noises everywhere. That's it. Goodnight noises everywhere.

EMERSON: Goodnight, Mom.

END OF PART THREE

reunion @ the fin de siecle
or: the return of the crazy guy
or: all things that do not return, return anyway

(There is something airborne about this segment, this play. The "scenes" as such flow in and out of one another without breaks.)

LIDDY: I thought about our reunion, me and the Crazy Guy. I planned it the year I loved him. I was sure it would happen on the subway in an old city. Some place foreign and old, older than California, older than what we remember. In 1999. Lovers on the edge of time.

STEPHEN: And then it did happen.

LIDDY: After years. Two or three of them. You found me. It wasn't at all like I thought.

(Lights up on STEPHEN)

STEPHEN: It did not take place on the subway. It did not take place in an old city. We met in a corporately owned bookstore in the Pacific Northwest. A relatively young city if you are familiar with the history and age of cities. There were no subways involved. No forms of public transportation at all. You had a car. I rode a bike. It was summer.

LIDDY: You found me, just like in fairy tales.

STEPHEN: We had both ended up in Seattle. You for your brother. Me, I'm not even really sure. You'd once said something about Seattle. For some reason, I ended

up here. Writing poems again. Working a job. It was okay, something I still didn't care too much about. But it was all okay. And I remember seeing you, noticing first the color of your hair, and then you—
Hello, Liddy Green.

LIDDY: Oh...

STEPHEN: From California. It's Stephen. How many years has it been?

LIDDY: Hi. *(Aside to audience)* [i attempt conversation but end up sounding more defensive than i mean to. it's just that, after two or three years, three really...]

STEPHEN: Scared?

LIDDY: Should I be scared?

STEPHEN: You still answer a question with a question. Don't you?

LIDDY: Do I? [liddy green recoups. recovers. remembers. oh my. it's the guy from the hospital. oh my.]

STEPHEN: How are you?

LIDDY: Do you live up here? [this strikes liddy green as a good conversation tactic]

STEPHEN: I do. Do you?

LIDDY: Yes.

STEPHEN: Funny.

LIDDY: Coincidence.

STEPHEN: If you believe in that kind of thing.

LIDDY: I do. Believe in that kind of thing. How are you? Did I ask that already?

STEPHEN: You do, huh?

LIDDY: Do what?

STEPHEN: Believe in that kind of thing.

LIDDY: How are you? Are you well?

STEPHEN: Yes. I am well.

LIDDY: Do you still...um...hear things?

STEPHEN: No. Do you?

LIDDY: No. How are you? Oh, I asked that.

STEPHEN: It's been a long time.

LIDDY: You were—

STEPHEN: Hospitalized.

LIDDY: Right.

STEPHEN: Well, eventually I got out. I wasn't there too long.

LIDDY: Of course. I was, um, I mean, after you, I had this—do you want to go somewhere and catch up?

STEPHEN: Absolutely. Can I buy you a coffee?

LIDDY: Absolutely.

STEPHEN: I'm unabashedly anxious—

LIDDY: What?

STEPHEN: To catch up.

LIDDY: Nobody says things like that except you.

STEPHEN: Things like what?

LIDDY: "Unabashedly anxious."

STEPHEN: Oh, you like that?

LIDDY: Didn't you know I would?

STEPHEN: Let me buy you a coffee.

LIDDY: *(To audience)* So we sat at a cafe. In the poetry section of a large corporately owned bookstore at the end of the century.

STEPHEN: The *fin de siecle*.

LIDDY: Fantasy Ecle?

STEPHEN: *Fin de siecle.* It means—

LIDDY: I know what it means.

STEPHEN: Of course you do. Here we are.

LIDDY: How are you? Did I ask that already?

STEPHEN: You did.

LIDDY: Oh.

STEPHEN: A couple of times.

STEPHEN: I want to hear everything. All of it. About you.

LIDDY: Oh. You mean like how I loved you so much that year and how long it took to let go of you and how I sort of just fell apart afterwards and found all sorts of demons that I didn't even know existed? Like that? Did you know I have a thing for tall lanky men from the East Coast who write poetry? You were the first. But there were others after you. Not all of them went to Yale.

STEPHEN: I guess I'm flattered.

LIDDY: Good.

(Beat. LIDDY *and* STEPHEN *smile. There is sexual tension.)*

(Lights up on EMERSON*)*

EMERSON: No, no no no no. This is wrong. This is not right. Would you agree? Liddy!?

LIDDY: I agree.

EMERSON: What section was he in? Mental health?

LIDDY: Poetry.

EMERSON: *(With disdain for poetry and mad poets)* Oh, God.

LIDDY: Reading Keats.

EMERSON: I don't want to know what happens next.

LIDDY: No. You probably don't.

EMERSON: Did you go somewhere with him?

LIDDY: Well. I did.

EMERSON: Don't tell me. Just don't.

LIDDY: Okay.

EMERSON: Where did you go!?

LIDDY: Just for coffee. I mean, after that first coffee, we met again, the next day. For more coffee. And we talked.

STEPHEN: And it rained.

LIDDY: It always rains.

STEPHEN: It's Seattle.

LIDDY: It's beautiful.

STEPHEN: You're beautiful.

LIDDY: Oh no. You can't do that.

STEPHEN: Do what?

LIDDY: You just can't.

STEPHEN: What?

LIDDY: Tell me I'm beautiful. You can't tell me I'm beautiful.

STEPHEN: Okay.

LIDDY: See, I am not at all the person I was when I thought I was in love with you. Many years have passed.

STEPHEN: Okay. Not that many, but okay.

LIDDY: I'm getting a refill. Do you want anything?

[i get a refill. i dont' even want one. i stopped drinking coffee a month ago but he just called me beautiful and i need a refill.] *(She gets a refill. Comes back the table)*

STEPHEN: What are you doing tomorrow? Want to meet me in Recovery and Addiction?

LIDDY: Okay.

visit #2

LIDDY: We met in the bookstore three times that week. And three times the next.

STEPHEN: Each day a different section.

LIDDY: Recovery and Addiction.

(The following are like fragments from a series of their conversations.)

LIDDY: I write articles now. Isn't that funny?

STEPHEN: I'm losing my hair. It comes out in chunks.

LIDDY: My background in clinical psychology is good. For articles.

STEPHEN: I'm still searching. I mean, I've done a lot of things since the hospital. But, I have to say, I think I"m still searching.

LIDDY: I understand something about people. About what happens inside of them. I'm still wondering how this might be a good thing. How it could be a gift.

STEPHEN: It's like, I chose something and in the choosing of it, committed myself to something a lot bigger than I thought. I chose a whole life not just six months in a hosptial. And it could have been a lot worse. I saw guys... I mean, it really could have messed me up.

LIDDY: It could have. I've changed a lot of my own ideas about mental health. What we construct around it.

STEPHEN: Me too.

Medication. Not an easy issue. It is not an easy one. When I take them...but when I don't take them.. but then, when I do. And on some level, I think I would prefer to feel that what I experienced was not a disorder. But more of a reordering. Anyway, there are studies being done with wheat gluten. Did you know that food allergies can be so severe as to mimic psychosis?

I do not hear voices anymore. Ever. I have nightmares sometimes—The meds make that stop. Most dreaming in fact stops when I'm on them. I'm not on them all the time.

LIDDY: My brother used to have nightmares. He doesn't anymore. Did you know my mom committed suicide when I was still in high school?

STEPHEN: I didn't. I'm sorry.

LIDDY: Yeah. Everyone says that.

STEPHEN: I'm sure they do.

LIDDY: Yeah.

STEPHEN: Yeah.

(Beat)

LIDDY: I went a little, well not crazy, but I went down. Not like you, of course. But after you, I let everything I'd built for myself, which wasn't a lot mind you, but anyway, I let it all crash. Which was good, kind of. I think I needed to break apart for a little while. And I just did. Break. I followed a spiral. Everything I thought was solid was not. It became liquid or worse, it became air. Everything underneath me evaporated and I was eighteen again and my mom was dead (and I didn't know who to call). I don't think I ever really grieved until...well, something about that day you said "don't". Something about that day you said don't. And, I didn't. Except I already had. And then it was too late. Way too late. And I evaporated. But then I came through it. I really did. And I moved up here to be closer to Em. Em's always single. I worry about him that way. I'm glad to be nearby.

STEPHEN: I want to touch you.

LIDDY: Excuse me?

STEPHEN: Remember?

LIDDY: Yes. I'm sorry about that. I—

STEPHEN: No. Please don't be. *(Beat)* I do, though. Now.

LIDDY: I have to go.

(LIDDY leaves the "scene" but now she and STEPHEN are talking to each other in a kind of future tense, commenting on what has gone by—)

STEPHEN: You are always the one to leave first. I'd like to point that out.

LIDDY: What was I supposed to do? Stay?

STEPHEN: Well. Sure.

LIDDY: That doesn't seem realistic to me.

STEPHEN: A lot of things do not seem realistic. Reality does not seem like it should mean a whole lot to people like you and me.

LIDDY: And what kind of people is that? Are we? And how do you know we are the same kind of people?

STEPHEN: Don't you think we are?

LIDDY: The jury is still out.

STEPHEN: When do they resume?

LIDDY: I don't know.

visits #3 and #4

STEPHEN: Well, I couldn't *fathom* what you were doing with me back then. It was really kind of messed up.

LIDDY: You were right. You said, "I can't." you were right.

STEPHEN: But now it's different, isn't it?

LIDDY: No.

STEPHEN: Why not?

LIDDY: Because. It isn't.

STEPHEN: It could be.

LIDDY: No it can't. You can't. It's too late, and you can't.

STEPHEN: Do you want to have coffee?

LIDDY: We can't keep having coffee.

STEPHEN: We can. It's Seattle.

LIDDY: You know what I mean.

STEPHEN: So lets go for a walk.

LIDDY: And we do. *(To him)*

STEPHEN: I missed you. I thought about you. But I also didn't.

LIDDY: I was madly in love with you.

STEPHEN: Interesting choice of adverbs. Madly denotes madness. Which is not wholly inappropriate. but which is, sort of, would you not say, ironic.

LIDDY: I've never dated an intellectual equal.

STEPHEN: Does that mean we're dating?

LIDDY: No. I just mean—

STEPHEN: Oh, you think we're equals?

LIDDY: Yes. Why? Don't you think you're as smart as me?

STEPHEN: I was wrong not to let you touch me.

LIDDY: No. You were not wrong. You were right.

visit #5

LIDDY: We finally kissed in front of New Nonfiction. In hardcover.

EMERSON: Liddy!

LIDDY: Well, I had to. It had been lurking for so long. Sometimes you have to do the thing you said you weren't going to do to know why you're not supposed to do it.

(LIDDY *goes to* STEPHEN. *Kisses him. They kiss passionately.*)

LIDDY: All the reasons why I can't:
Mental illness
The past
The future
My brother would kill me
My mom would turn over in her grave
Mental illness— Okay, I guess that's the biggest one.

(*From here to the end of the play is collaged, in and out— towards the end of the sequence the lines start to run on top of one another so that when* STEPHEN *says "Come here", he breaks through something.*)

LIDDY: I want to touch you.

STEPHEN: Why?

LIDDY: Why? Because I do.

STEPHEN: Don't.

LIDDY: But I do. And it's too late because my hand is already reaching which means my heart has already decided.

EMERSON: My mother killed herself during the second semester of my sophomore year at Stanford. I was dating a girl called Susan, and I had just begun to meditate. I was dating a girl called Carla. No, that was the meditation teacher. I never dated her. I did kiss her once. But I was dating Susan, living with her, really. Until we broke up. I think she's married now.

STEPHEN: I couldn't fathom what you were doing with me.

EMERSON: To a judge. She's married to a judge.

STEPHEN: We were taught reality is subjective.

LIDDY: There are secrets and you don't know them, and I want to touch you.

STEPHEN: I was wrong. And I want you to now.

LIDDY: We could break him out and move to Seattle.

EMERSON: Okay, no.

LIDDY: Okay, all the reasons why I can't. One, you said don't. Two, my brother said no. But mostly, one, you said don't.

STEPHEN: I was wrong.

LIDDY: I have been waiting to hold you for years. Thinking about it. And waiting.

EMERSON: All the reasons I can't—

STEPHEN: I want to—

LIDDY: I do too—

STEPHEN: Good.

LIDDY: But I can't. Want to. But can't.

STEPHEN: Come here—

(LIDDY *sits on* STEPHEN's *lap. She's quiet. Everything is quiet.*)

STEPHEN: I like you like this. Quiet.

(STEPHEN *reaches for* LIDDY. *She pulls away.*)

LIDDY: It's complicated.

STEPHEN: Sure.

(LIDDY *kisses* STEPHEN.)

LIDDY: How do you bring the past and present together without disastrous results?

STEPHEN: There might be disastrous results.

LIDDY: Yes. There might be.

STEPHEN: Yes. there might be.

LIDDY: And then what?

STEPHEN: We don't know.

LIDDY: Oh my.

END OF PLAY